FOR ORGANS, PIANOS & ELECTRONIC KEYBOARDS

E-Z PLAY® TODAY

376

BILLY JOEL

River of Dreams

Y0-DDP-194

Cover Art: Christie Brinkley

ISBN 0-7935-3145-4

HAL•LEONARD
CORPORATION
7777 W. BLUEMOUND RD. P.O. BOX 13819 MILWAUKEE, WI 53213

CONTENTS

All About Soul

Registration 8
Rhythm: Rock or Pops

Words and Music by
Billy Joel

She waits for me at night, she
peo - ple who have lost

waits for me in si - lence. She
trace of hu - man kind - ness. There are

gives me all her ten - der - ness
man - y who have fal - len, there are

and takes a - way my pain. And
some who still sur - vive. She

so far she has-n't run, though I swear she's had her
comes to me ____ at night and she tells me her de -

mo - ments, she still be - lieves in mir - a - cles
sires and she gives me all the love I need

while oth - ers cry in vain. It's all a - bout soul.
to keep my faith a - live. It's all a - bout soul.

It's all a - bout faith and a deep - er de - vo -
It's all a - bout joy that comes ____ out of sor -

tion. It's all a - bout soul _____
row. It's all a - bout soul, _____

'cause un - der the love is a strong - er e - mo -
who's stand - ing now and who's stand - ing to - mor -

tion. She's got to be strong_____
row. You've got to be hard,_____

'cause so man - y things get - ting out of con -
hard as the rock in that old rock 'n'

trol should drive her a - way. So, why does she stay?
roll, but that's on - ly part, you know in your heart

It's all a - bout soul._____
it's all a - bout soul._____

She

turns to me some - times and she asks me what I'm dream-
ask her how she knew to reach out for me at that

ing and I re - al - ize
moment and she smiles be - cause

I must have gone
it's un - der - stood

a mil - lion miles ___ a - way. And I
there are no words ___ to say. It's

all a - bout soul. ___ It's all a - bout

know - ing what some - one is feel - ing. The wom - an's got soul, _____ the pow - er of

love and the pow - er of heal - ing. This life is - n't

fair. _____ It's gon - na get dark,

it's gon - na get cold. You've got to get

tough, but that ain't e - nough. It's all a - bout

soul.

Ah, _____ na na na na na na na na.

It's all a - bout soul. _____ Na na na

na na na na. Yes, it is. _____

Na na na na na na na na. It's

10

all a-bout soul. _____

D.S. al Coda
(Return to 𝄉
Play to ⨁ and
Skip to Coda)

CODA
⨁

There are

Oh, ___ yeah, oh. ___ Na na na na na na na.

It's all a-bout soul. _____ Na na

Repeat and Fade

na na na na na. Yes, it is. _____

The Great Wall Of China

Registration 2
Rhythm: Rock

Words and Music by
Billy Joel

Ad - vice is cheap, you can take it from me. _____
You take a piece of what - ev - er you touch. ___

It's yours to keep 'cause o - pin - ions are free. _____
Too man - y pieces means you're touch - ing too much. _____

No - bod - y knows 'bout the trou - ble I've seen. _____
You nev - er win if you can't play it straight. _____

No - bod - y's per - fect, mis - ter, no - bod - y's clean.
You on - ly beat me if you get me to hate.

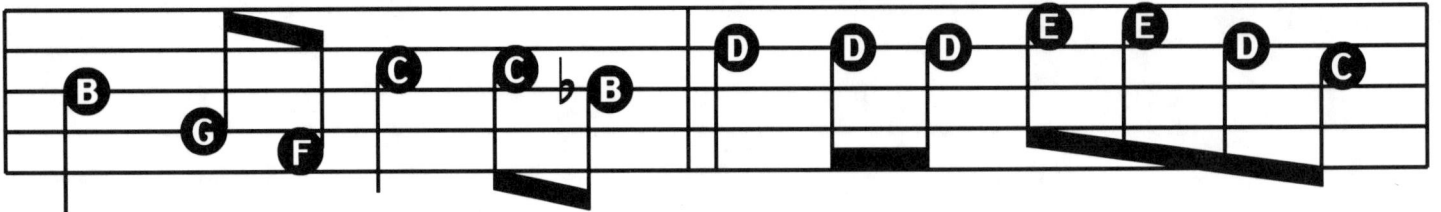

It costs too much and takes too long to find out too late.
It must be so lone - ly to think that you have on - ly
This was not your call - ing, just look how far you've fal - len.

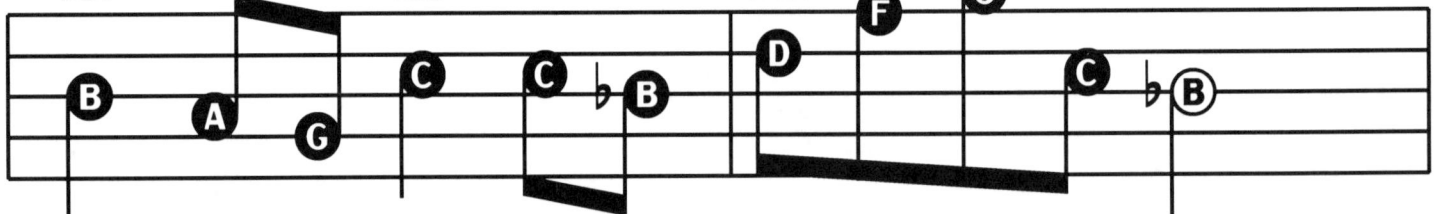

Some words are not heard 'til af - ter they're spo - ken.
some - bod - y else's life to live if they let you.
I heard your story, man, you've got to be jok - ing.

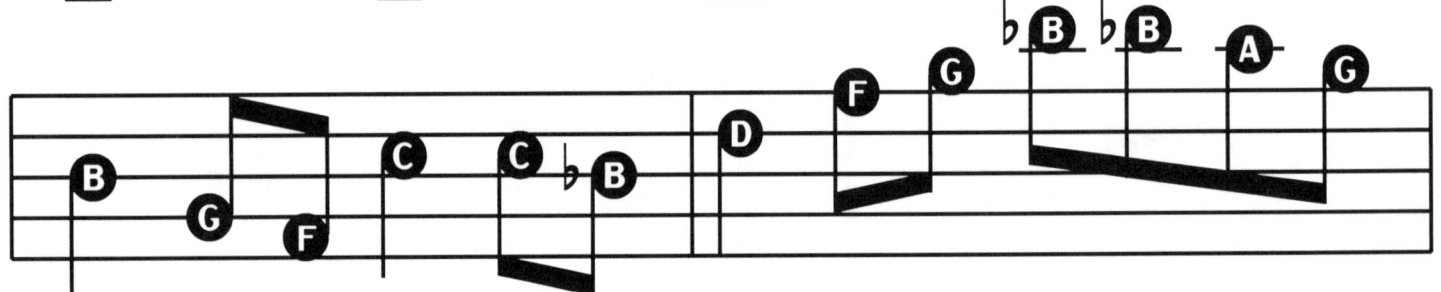

Your role was pro - tec - tive, your soul was too de - fec - tive.
I ain't too se - lec - tive, but it don't take no de - tec - tive
Keep things in per - spec - tive, this is my true ob - jec - tive.

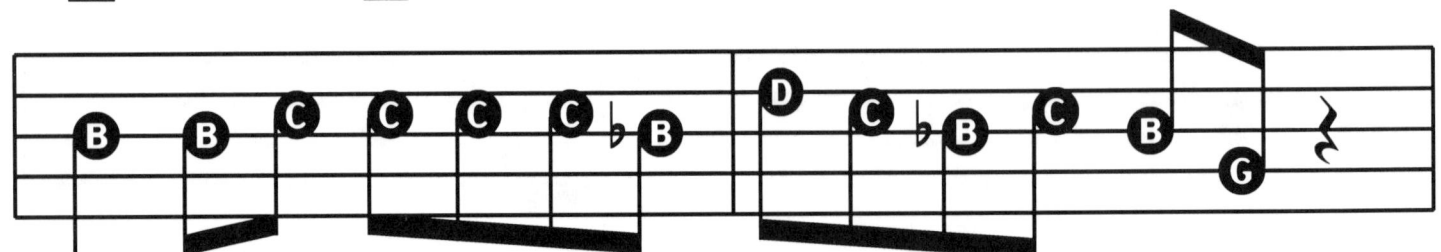

Some peo - ple just don't have a heart to be bro - ken. ____
to find out how fast your friends will for - get you. ____
Why tear this heart out if it's on - ly been bro - ken? ____

C

E E E E E E E E E E F E F E

3　　　　　　*3*

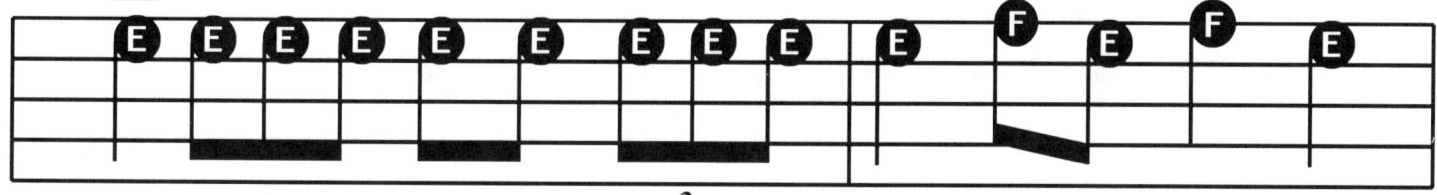

(1.,3.) We could have gone all the way to the Great Wall of Chi - na
(2.) We could have gone all the way to the Great Wall of Chi - na.

F　　　　　　　　C　　　　　　Ab　　Db

A C C C C C C C C A C

3　　*3*　　*3*

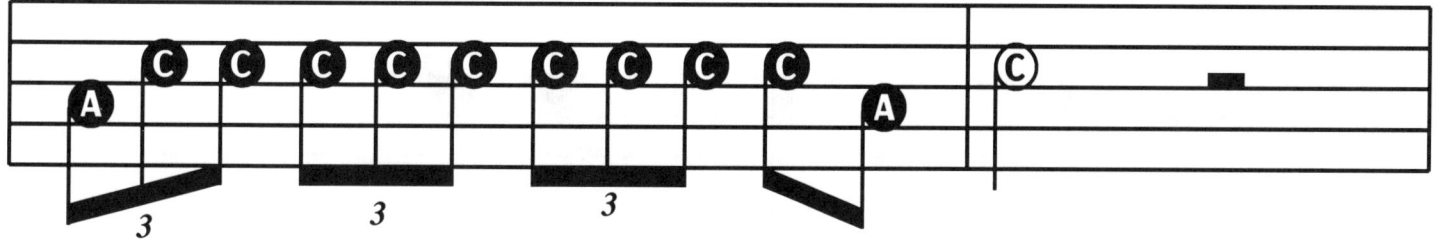

if you'd on - ly had a lit - tle more faith in me,
Now all you're go - ing to be is his - to - ry.

C

E E E E E E E E E F G F E D

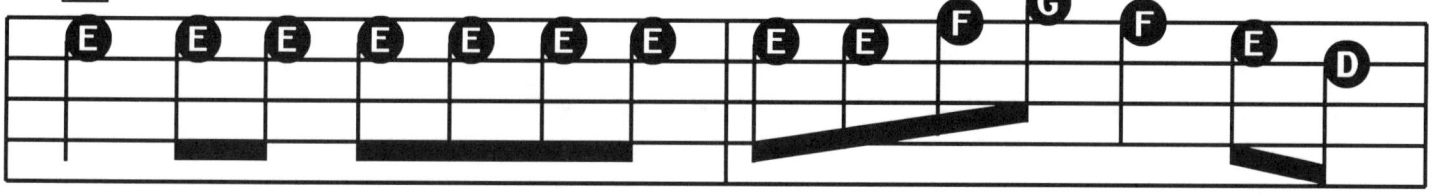

in lieu of dia - monds, gold and plat - i - num re - mind - ers will
Help yourself, it's all you can eat at the Em - pire _____ Di - ner to -

F　　　　　　C　　　　　　D

C C A

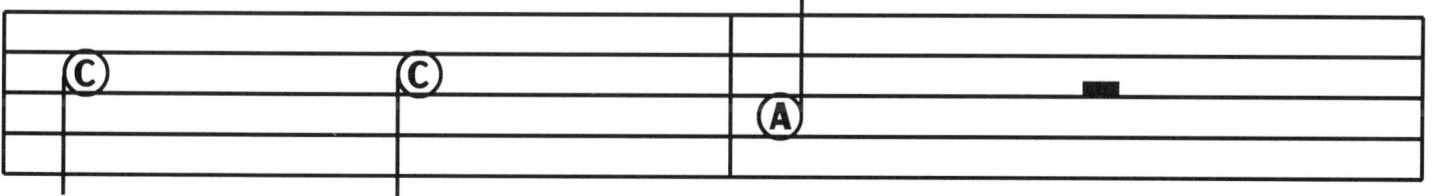

still shine bright.
night._____

C

E E E E. C E F G F E C

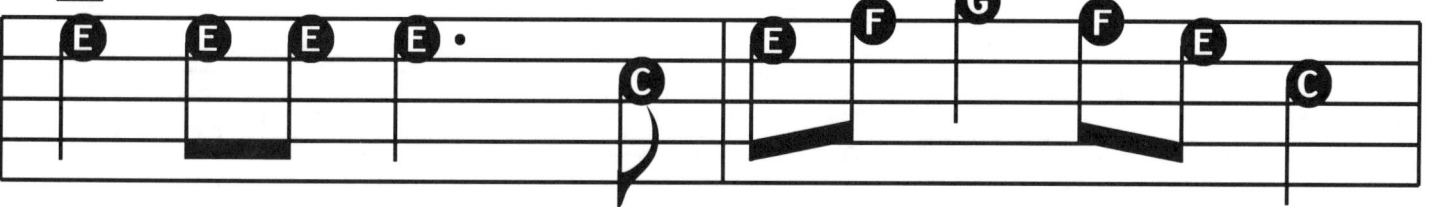

All the king's men and all the king's hors - es can't
You coulda had class, you could have been a con - tend - er.

14

D.S. al Coda
(Return to %
Play to ⊕ and
Skip to Coda)

ah, _____ ah. _____

CODA

na. _____

Ah, _____ ah; _____

ah, _____ ah. _____

Blonde Over Blue

Registration 7
Rhythm: Rock

Words and Music by
Billy Joel

C

C G G A | B C G G A

Some days when I'm far a - way in a
These days when there's a mil - lion ways to be
These days not a damn soul prays and there

F

B A F G A | B A F G

lone - ly room in a cold se - clu - sion;
pulled and torn, to be mis - di - rect - ed.
is no faith, 'cause there's noth - ing to be - lieve in.

C

C G G A | B C G G A

some nights when I'm wound so tight there is
These times when there are sins and crimes on is
These days on - ly good luck pays if we

F

B A F | B A F | B A G

no re - lease, there is no so - lu - tion.
morn - ing shows for the dis - con - nect - ed.
don't get paid then we try to get e - ven.

C

In hell there's a big ho - tel where the
I look and I write my book and I
I look and I write my book and I

F

bar just closed and the win - dows nev - er o - pened.
walk a - way with the wrong im - pres - sions.
have my say and I draw con - clu - sions.

C

No phone, so you can't call home and the
I don't care 'cause I've done my share and I
Some nights when I'm wound so tight, there is

F

T. V. works, but the click - er is bro - ken.
need some time for my own ob - ses - sions,
no re - lease, for there is no sol - u - tion.

Eb ... **Bb** ... **F**

G Bb D | D ... C

But in the dark - ness,
It does - n't mat - ter,
But in the dark - ness,

Eb ... **F**

G Bb bE | G F ... C

I see your light turned on.
I've let that life go by.
I see your light turned on.

Eb ... **Bb** ... **F**

G Bb D | D ... C

You know my weak - ness,
It's been for - got - ten,
You know my weak - ness,

Eb ... **F**

G Bb bE | G F C D

you know how I re - spond to ____
'cause all I want - ed was you, ____
you know how I re - spond to ____

G · · · **D** · · **C**

blonde o - ver blue.
blonde o - ver blue.
blonde o - ver blue. } Your hands are cold, your

G · · · · **D**

eyes are fire. _____ Blonde o - ver blue, they___

C · · · **F** · **G**

_____ shine as though you're burn - ing in - side. One word from

D · · **C** · · · **G**

you is all I need to be in - spired._____

To Coda ⊕ **D** · · · · **C**

Blonde o - ver blue, I_____ need your in - spir -

1

G F C

a - tion to - night.

2

F C

D.C. al Coda
(Return to beginning
Play to ⬙ and
Skip to Coda)

night.

CODA

D C F

blue, I need your in - spir - a - tion to - night.

G D C

Blonde o - ver blue, your hands are cold, your

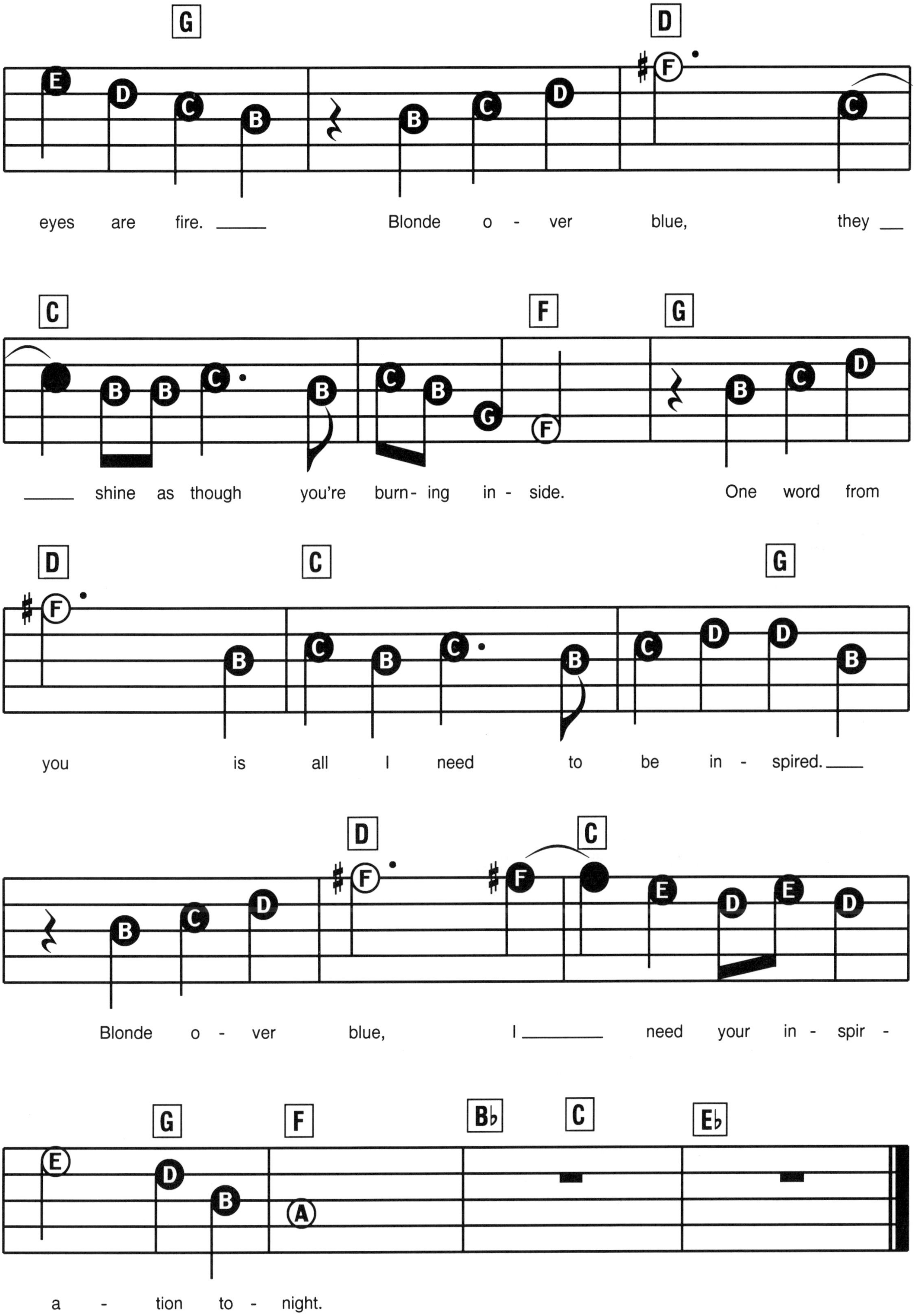
G D
eyes are fire. Blonde o - ver blue, they
C F G
shine as though you're burn- ing in - side. One word from
D C G
you is all I need to be in - spired.
D C
Blonde o - ver blue, I need your in - spir -
G F B♭ C E♭
a - tion to - night.

Famous Last Words

Registration 5
Rhythm: Rock

Words and Music by
Billy Joel

Sit - ting here in Av - a - lon,
There's com - fort in my cof - fee cup
(D.C.) *Instrumental solo*

look - ing at the pour - ing rain,_____
and ap - ples in the ear - ly fall. _____

sum - mer - time has come and gone,_____
they're pull - ing all the moor - ings up _____

and ev - 'ry - bod - y's home a - gain. _____
and gath - 'ring at the Le - gion Hall. _____
Solo ends

23

G

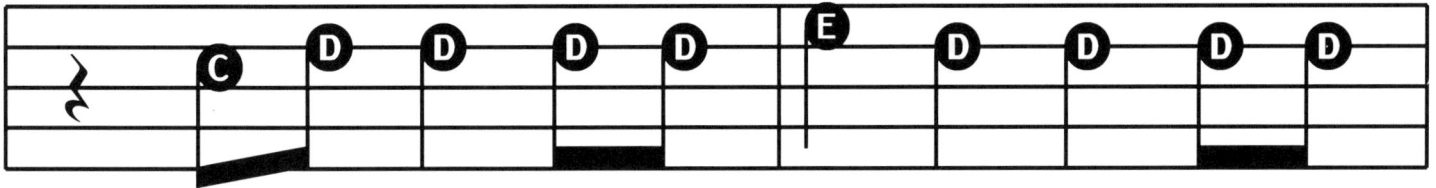

Closing down for the sea - son, I found the
They swept a - way all the stream - ers af - ter the
Stack the chairs on the ta - ble tops, hang the

B♭　　　　　　**F**

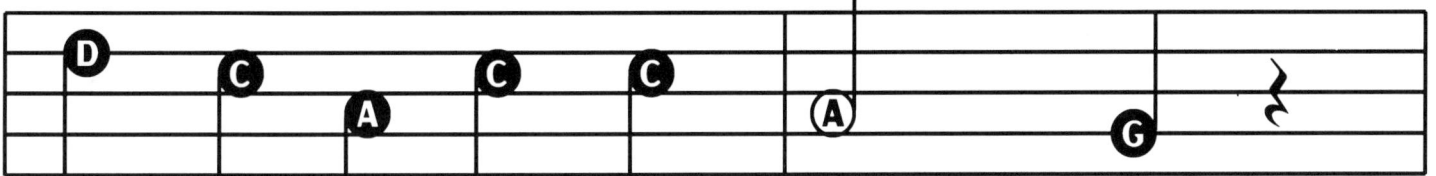

last of the sou - ve - nirs. _____
La - bor Day _____ pa - rade. _____
sheets on the chan - de - liers. _____

G

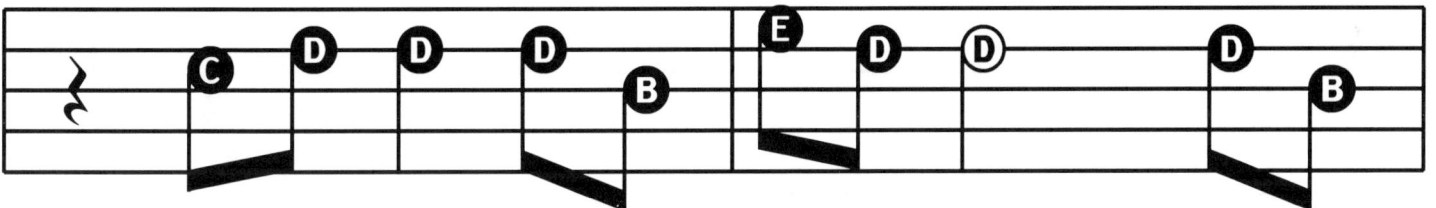

I can still taste the wed - ding cake and it's
Noth - ing left for a dream - er now, on - ly
It slows down, but it nev - er stops, ain't it

Am7
Am　　　　　　**B♭**　　　　**To Coda**

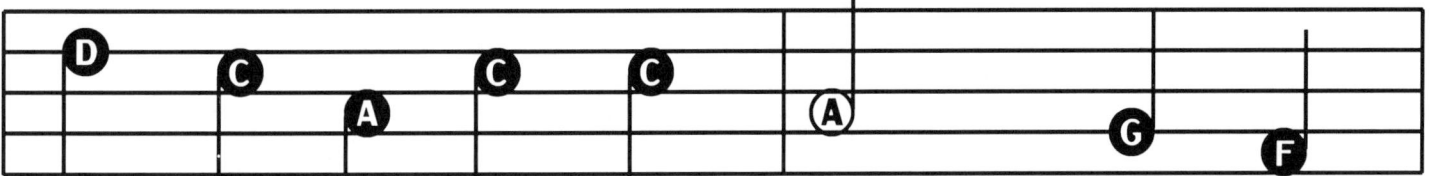

sweet af - ter all these years. _____
one fi - nal ser - e - nade. _____
sweet af - ter all these years. _____

These are the last words I have to say, _____
And these are the last words I have to say, _____

_____
_____

that's why this took so long to
be - fore an - oth - er age goes

write. _____
by _____

There will be
with all those

oth - er words some oth - er ___ day, _____
oth - er songs I'll have ___ to play, _____

but that's the sto - ry of my _____ life.
but that's the

sto - ry of my ____ life. And it's so

clear stand - ing here where I _____ am. _____

Ain't that what jus - tice is

F ... **Fm**

for? _____ Frank - ly, my

E♭ ... **B♭** ... **F**

D.C. al Coda
(Return to beginning
Play to ⊕ and
Skip to Coda)

dear, _____ I don't give a damn an - y - more.

CODA ⊕ **F** ... **B♭**

And these are the last words I
These are the last words I
These are the last words I

C ... **B♭**

have to say. _____
have to say, _____
have to say _____

It's always hard to say good - bye, _____
that's why it took so long to write. _____
be - fore an - oth - er age goes by _____

but now it's time to put this
There will be oth - er words some
with all those oth - er songs I'll

book a - way. _____ Ain't that the
oth - er _____ day. _____ Ain't that the
have _____ to play. _____ Ain't that the

Repeat and Fade

sto - ry of my _____ life.
sto - ry of my _____ life.
sto - ry of my _____ life.

Lullabye
(Goodnight, My Angel)

Registration 3
Rhythm: 8 Beat or Pops

Words and Music by
Billy Joel

G ... **Cm** **G**

B B A A B B C C· B B

Good - night, my an - gel, time to close your eyes,
Good - night, my an - gel, now it's time to sleep,

D7 / **D** **Em** **D** **C**

A A A A G G #F #F· E E

and save these ques - tions for an - oth - er day.
and still so man - y things I want to say.

G **Cm** **G**

B B A A B B C C· B B

I think I know what you've been ask - ing me.
Re - mem - ber all the songs you sang for me

D7 / **D** **Em** **D** **A**

A A A A G G #F #F· E E

I think you know what I've been try - ing to say.
when we went sail - ing on an em - 'rald bay.

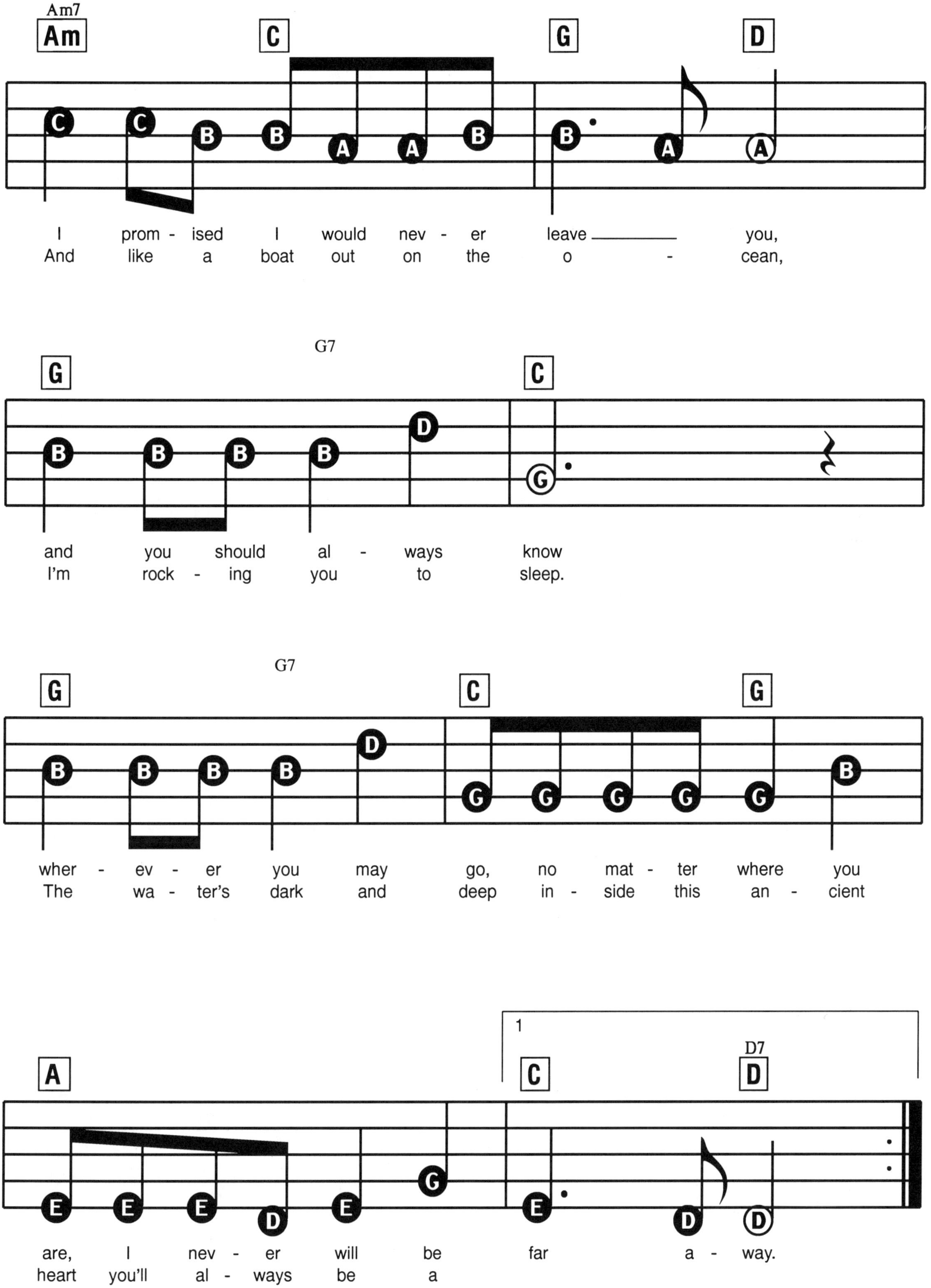

2

C | **D** | **G**

E. part
D of
D me.

B Good -
B night,
A my
A an -
B gel,
B now
C it's

Cm | **G** | **D** (D7) | **Em**

C. time
B to
B dream,

A and
A dream
A how
A won -
G der -
G ful
#F your

D | **C** | **G**

#F. life
E will
E be.

B Some -
B day
A your
A child
B may
B cry,
D and

C | **A** | **Cm** | **G**

D if
C you
C sing
B this
B lul -
A la -
A bye,

A then
B in
C your
D heart
B there
G will

al - ways be a part of me.

Some - day we'll all be gone but lul - la - byes go on and on.

They nev - er die, that's how you and _____ I will

be. _____

A Minor Variation

Registration 5
Rhythm: 8 Beat or Pops

Words and Music by
Billy Joel

Line 1 (F7 / F, Bbm, Bbm7)

Notes: A A G F E | A G F F G A

Some days I have to give right _____ in to the
When trou - bles want to find me, I ain't hard to
I'm get - ting to the point where I don't feel the

Line 2 (F7 / F, Bbm, Bbm7)

Notes: F D C | B D F G A

blues. _____
find. _____
pain, _____
De - spite how I try
They know where I am,
and I've had e - nough.

Line 3 (F7 / F, Bbm, Bbm7)

Notes: A A G F E | A G F G A

to keep fight - in', it's a sure shot I'm going to
like a hun - gry pack for the wolves when it's feed - ing
I'm read - y for the next time it hits me a -

Line 4 (D7 / D, Bbm, Bbm7)

Notes: F D C | B D F G

lose, _____
time, _____
gain, _____
and I'll tell you
they tear up a
'cause I've got - ten

Dm7
Dm
why. You think I'm cra - zy.
man. And it's a strange thing
tough. It does - n't faze me
E♭
It's such a sad com - po - si - tion.
'cause now it don't real - ly mat - ter.
and now I've made my de - ci - sion.
Dm7
Dm
But can you blame me
More of the same thing
I may be cra - zy.
D♭
for what's been caus - ing my bad dis - po - si - tion?
don't e - ven hurt, it's a part of the pat - tern.
It's not as though I don't know that con - di - tion.

34

Ain't noth - ing new with my blue sit - u - a - tion,
But still in all it's a small con - so - la - tion.
Un - til I'm through with this blue sit - u - a - tion,

and noth - ing's fine, it's just a mi - nor var - i - a - tion.
I just de - fine it as a mi - nor var - i - a - tion.
pass me the wine, it's just a mi - nor var - i - a - tion.

Uh!

Ain't no way to fight 'em dar - ling.
Ain't no - bod - y's busi - ness, ba - by.

Ain't no way a - round 'em, ba - by.
Ain't no - bod - y's wor - ry, dar - lin'.

Ain't no way to take 'em.
Ain't no - bod - y's prob - lem.

No - where to hide and, be - lieve me, I've tried to shake 'em.
No way to win when you've

2

Dm7 | **Dm**

al - read - y been for - got - ten. And it's a

E♭

strange thing, 'cause now it

Dm7 | **Dm**

don't real - ly mat - ter. More of the

D♭

same thing don't e - ven hurt, it's a

part of the pat - tern. Un - til I'm through with this

blue sit - u - a - tion, pass me the wine, it's just

mi - nor var - i - a - tion.

Mi - nor var - i - a - tion.

Repeat and Fade

The River Of Dreams

Registration 8
Rhythm: Shuffle, Blues, or Swing

Words and Music by
Billy Joel

In the mid - dle of the night _____
night _____

I go walk - ing in my sleep, _____
I go walk - ing in my sleep, _____

from the moun - tains of faith
through the val - ley of fear

to a riv - er so deep. _____
to a riv - er so deep. _____

G

I must be look - ing for some - thing, _____
And I've been search - ing for some - thing, _____

some - thing sa - cred I lost. _____
tak - en out of my soul, _____

C

But the riv - er is wide
some - thing I would never lose

D

and it's too hard to cross. _____
some - thing some - bod - y stole. _____

Em

_____
_____

And e - ven though I know the
I don't know why I go

D **C**

riv - er is wide I walk down ev - 'ry eve - ning and
walk - ing at night but now I'm tired and I don't want to

Bm7 **Bm** **C**

stand on the shore, and try to cross to the
walk an - y - more. I hope it doesn't take the

Bm7 **Bm** **1** **A**

op - po - site side so I can fi - nal - ly find what I've been
rest of my life un - til I

D

look - ing for. In the mid - dle of the

2

A   **D**

B A A A   E D   E D D

find what it is I've been look - ing for.

D D E D B A

In the mid - dle of the

G

B A G   D D D D B A

night, _____ I go walk - ing in my
night, _____ I go walk - ing in my

A G   E D E D C

sleep, ____ through the jun - gle of
sleep, ____ through the des - ert of

C

C   E D E D D

doubt   to a riv - er so
truth   to a riv - er so

42

D

deep. _____   I   know   I'm   search - ing   for
deep. _____   We   all   end   in   the

G

some - thing, _____   some - thing   so   un - de -
o - cean, _____   we   all   start   in   the

fined _____   that   it   can   hard - ly   be
streams. _____   We're   all   car - ried   a -

C

seen _____   by   the   eyes   of   the
long _____   by   the   riv - er   of

To Coda ⊕

D

blind, _____   in   the   mid - dle   of   the
dreams, _____   in   the   mid - dle   of   the

night. _____ I'm not sure a - bout a

life af - ter this, God knows I've nev - er been a

spir - it - ual man. Bap - tized by the

fire, I wade in - to the riv - er that runs to the

prom - ised land.

D.S. al Coda
(Return to 𝄋
Play to ⊕ and
Skip to Coda)

In the mid - dle of the

CODA ⊕ G

night. I go walk- ing in the, in the mid - dle of the;

I go walk - ing in the, in the mid - dle of the;

C

I go walk - ing in the, in the mid - dle of the;

D

I go walk - ing in the, in the mid - dle of the;

G

I go walk - ing in the, in the mid - dle of the;

I go walk - ing in the, in the mid - dle of the;

C

I go walk - ing in the, in the mid - dle of the;

Repeat and Fade

D

I go walk - ing in the, in the mid - dle of the;

Shades Of Grey

Registration 1
Rhythm: Pop, 8 Beat, or Rock

Words and Music by
Billy Joel

Ba ba ba du wop bop ba ba du wop bop

ba ba du wa da. _____ Ba ba ba du wop bop

ba ba du wop bop ba ba du wa da. _____

Some things were per - fect - ly clear,
Once there were trench - es and walls,
Now with the wis - dom of years,

C ... **Bm** ... **Em**

C C C B A G G E

seen with the vi - sion of youth. _____
and one with point of ev - 'ry view. _____
I try to rea - son things out, _____

D

G G A F# E D E D

No doubts and noth - ing to _____ fear,
Fight 'til and the oth - er man _____ falls.
and the on - ly peo - ple I _____ fear

C ... **Bm** ... **Em**

C C C B A G G

I claimed the cor - ner on truth.
Kill him be - fore he kills you.
are those who nev - er have doubts.

D

G G. A F# E D E D

These days, it's hard - er to _____ say,
These days, the edg - es are _____ blurred.
Save us all from ar - ro - gant_____ men,

C ... **Bm** ... **Em**

I know what I'm fight - ing for. _____
I'm old and tir - ed of war. _____
and all the caus - es they're for. _____

D ... **C**

My faith is fall - ing a - way. ⎫
I hear the oth - er man's___ words. ⎬ I'm not that
I won't be right - eous a - gain. ⎭

D ... **G** ... **C** ... **D**

sure an - y - more. _____

G ... **C** ... **D** ... **G** ... To Coda ⊕ ... **C**

⎧ Shades of grey wher -
⎨ Shades of grey are

Em | D | G | C

ev - er I go, the | more I find out, the
all that I find, | when I look to the

D | Em | G | C

less that I _____ know. | Black and white is
en - e - my _____ line. | Black and white was so

Em | D | G | C

how it should be, ⎫ | but shades of grey are the
eas - y for me, ⎭ |

D | E | **1** Em | **2** Em

D.S. al Coda
(Return to ℅
Play to ⊕ and
Skip to Coda)

col - ors I _____ see. _____ | Ba _____ | Ba

CODA

G · C · Em · D

Shades of grey wher - ev - er I go, the

G · C · D · Em

more I find out, the less that I _____ know. There

G · C · Em · D

ain't no rain - bows shin - ing on me.

G · C · D · Em

1

Shades of grey are the col - ors I _____ see.

2

| D | E | Em |

col - ors I_____ see. _____ Ba

| C | G | C |

ba ba du wop bop ba ba du wop bop

1

| Bm | Em |

ba ba du wa da. _____ Ba

2

| Bm | E |

ba ba da wa da. _____

Two Thousand Years

Registration 8
Rhythm: Waltz

Words and Music by
Billy Joel

In the be - gin - ning
mo - ment,
mira - cles,

there was the cold and the night.
here at the cross - roads of time.
af - ter the last war is won.

Gm   Gm7 / Gm

Pro - phets and an - gels
We hope our chil - dren
Sci - ence and poet - ry

gave us the fire and the light.
car - ry our dreams down the line.
rule in the new world to come.

53

E♭

D7 / D **Gm**

F

B♭ **C**

Man   was   tri - um - phant, _____
They   are   the   vin - tage, _____
Pro - phets   and   an - gels _____

armed   with   the   faith   and   the   will
what   kind   of   life   will   they   to   live?
gave   us   the   pow - er   they   to   see.

that   e - ven   the   dark -
Is   this   a   curse
What   an   a - maz -

est   ag - es _____ could - n't   kill. _____
or   a   bless - ing _____ that   we   give? _____
ing   fu - ture _____ there   will   be. _____

Too man - y king - doms.
Some - times I won - der
And in the eve - ning,

Too man - y flags
why are we so
af - ter we the fire

on the field. So man - y bat - tles,
blind to fate? With - out com - pas - sion,
and the light, one thing is cer - tain:

so man - y wounds
there can be no
noth - ing can hold

C
F
E♭
to be healed. Time is re - lent - less.
end to hate, no end to sor - row,
back the night. Time is re - lent - less.
D7
D
On - ly true love
caused by the same
And to the past
Gm
per - se - veres.
end - less fears.
dis - ap - pears,
To Coda
F
Dm
It's been a long time and now,
Why can't we learn from all
we're on the

I'm with you,
we've been through,

af - ter
af - ter

two _____ thou - sand years. _____
two _____ thou - sand years. _____

This is our There will be

D.S. al Coda
(Return to %
Play to ⊕ and
Skip to Coda)

CODA

verge   of   all

things   new.   We are ———— two

thou - sand   years. ————

————

No Man's Land

Registration 5
Rhythm: Rock

Words and Music by
Billy Joel

Em

E E E — **G** — E D D. — E

I've seen those big ma - chines come
There ain't much work out here in
I see these chil - dren with their

D

E D D. D — **A** — D ♯C ♯C

roll - ing through the qui - et pines,
our con - sum - er their pow - er base,
bore - dom and their va - cant stares.

Em

E E E — **G** E D E E

blue suits and bank - ers with their
no ma - jor in - dus - try, just
God help us all if we're to

D

E D D ♯F — **A** ♯F E E

Vol - vos and their val - en - tines.
miles and miles of park - ing space.
blame for their un - an - swered prayers.

Em   **G**

Give us this day our dai - ly
This morn - ing's pa - per says our
They roll the side - walks up at

D   **A**

dis - count out - let mer - chan - dise.
neigh - bor's in a co - caine bust.
night, this place goes un - der - ground.

Em   **G**

Raise up a mul - ti - plex and
Lots more to read a - bout, Lo -
Thanks more to the Con - do Kings there's

D   **A**

we will make a sac - ri - fice.
li - ta make and sub - ur - ban lust.
ca - ble now in Zom - bie - town.

B ... **A**

Now we're gon - na get the big bus - 'ness.
Now we're gon - na get the whole sto - ry.
Now we're gon - na get the closed cir - cuit.

B ... **A** ... **B** ... To Coda ⊕

Now we're gon - na get the real thing. Ev - 'ry - bod - y's all ex -
Now we're gon - na be in prime time. Ev - 'ry - bod - y's all ex -
Now we're gon - na get the Top Forty. Now we're gon - na get the

C

cit - ed a - bout it. Who re - mem - bers when it
cit - ed a - bout it. Who re - mem - bers when it

G ... **D**

all be - gan out here in
all be - gan out here in

No Man's Land? _____   Be - fore they passed the
No Man's Land? _____   We've just be - gun to

mas - ter plan ____ }
un - der - stand ____ }   out here in No Man's Land. ____

Low sup - ply   and high de - mand   here in No Man's

Land, _____

{ in No Man's Land.
{ here in No Man's Land.

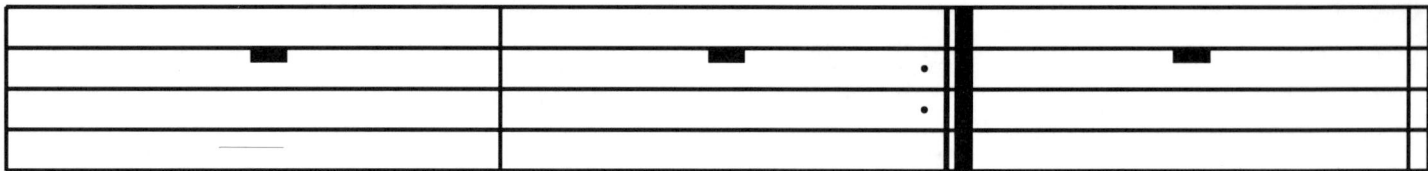

D.C. al Coda
(Return to beginning
Play to ⊕ and
Skip to Coda)

CODA

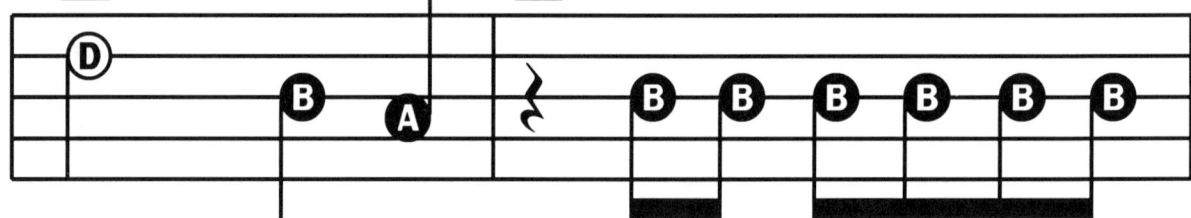

sports   fran - chise.   Now we're gon - na   get   the

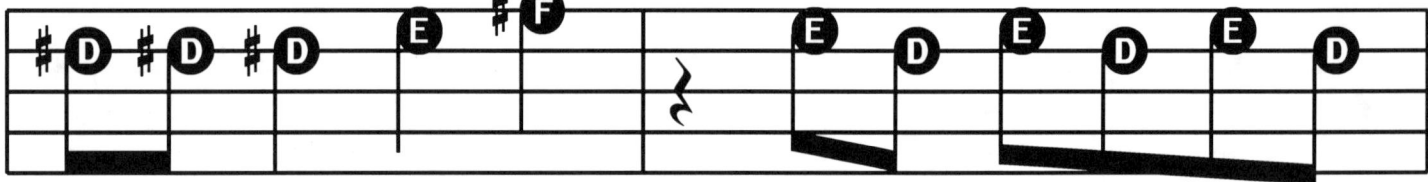

ma - jor   at - trac - tions.   Who re - mem - bers   when   it

all   be - gan   out   here   in

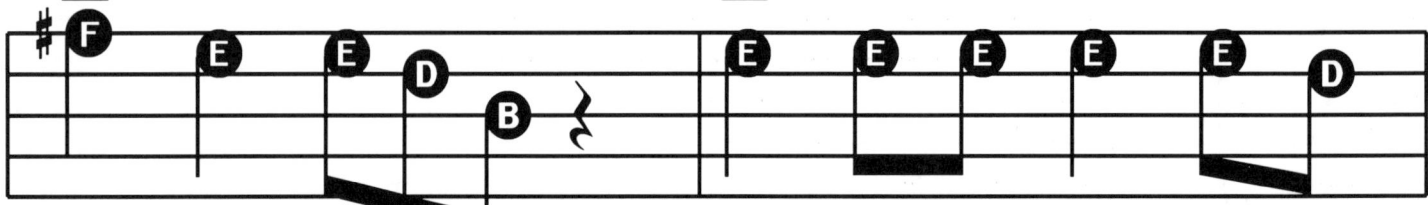

No   Man's   Land?_____   Be - fore   the   whole   world   was in our hands___ out here in

No Man's Land;___ be - fore the ban - ners and the

march - ing bands out here in

No Man's Land; ___ low sup - ply,

high de - mand here in No Man's

Land;

here in No Man's Land;

here in No Man's Land;

Repeat and Fade

here in No Man's